Seven Prir

GOOD MENTAL HEALTH

By the same author

When Time Is at a Premium: Cognitive-Behavioural Approaches to Single-Session Therapy and Very Brief Coaching (2016)

Attitudes in Rational Emotive Behaviour Therapy (REBT): Components, Characteristics and Adversity-related Consequences (2016)

Seven Principles of
GOOD MENTAL HEALTH

Windy Dryden, PhD

Rationality Publications

Rationality Publications
136 Montagu Mansions, London W1U 6LQ

www.rationalitypublications.com
info@rationalitypublications.com

First edition published by Rationality Publications
Copyright (c) 2021 Windy Dryden

The right of Windy Dryden to be identified as the author of
this work has been asserted in accordance with sections 77
and 78 of the Copyright Designs and Patents Act 1988.

A catalogue record of this book is
available from the British Library.

First edition 2021

ISBN: 978-1-910301-86-9

Contents

Introduction

In this short book, I plan to outline seven principles that underpin good mental health. In doing so, I want to stress that, in my opinion, a person demonstrates good mental health not by being happy or by having a sunny disposition. Instead, they demonstrate this by how they respond to the many adversities that they will experience as they navigate the difficult journey through this wondrous thing called life. It is doubtful that any of us can live a life free from adversity. Who of us can say, for example, that we have never encountered failure, rejection, and negative behaviour from others, to name but a few of the adversities that are likely to befall us?

The first principle that I will discuss in this book concerns you taking personal responsibility for your responses towards the adversities you may face. This is particularly the case when you disturb yourself about such adversities. If you think that the adversities you encounter make you disturbed, you will not do anything to change yourself. You will believe that the only way you can help yourself is to withdraw from these adversities so that you do not face them. This may be fine if you can avoid them, but you will consider yourself hopeless to effect change if you can't.

This book is based on the ideas of an American clinical psychologist, Dr Albert Ellis (1913–2007), who established an approach to counselling and psychotherapy in the mid-1950s known as 'Rational Emotive Behaviour Therapy' (REBT). REBT can be best placed within the cognitive-behavioural therapeutic tradition and was the first approach to CBT to be developed. One of the influences on Ellis's thoughts was the writings of the Greek Stoic philosopher, Epictetus, whose quote, 'Men are disturbed not by things, but by the view that they take of them', became many years later the cornerstone of REBT. In this book, I use the term 'attitude' rather than 'view' and restate Epictetus's position thus: 'People are not disturbed by life's adversities. Rather they disturb themselves about these adversities by the attitudes that they hold towards them.' This position clearly shows that while an adversity may contribute to your disturbance (after all, if the adversity did not exist, you would not be disturbed), it is the attitudes you take towards the adversity that are the prime determinants of your disturbed feelings. And since these attitudes are yours, you can be said to be responsible for them.

In some ways, if you don't grasp what I call in this book 'Principle 1' you probably won't get much from the rest of the book, although some people who don't accept the responsibility principle initially may grasp it later when they read the rest of the book. So don't be overly concerned if you struggle to accept 'Principle 1' on initial reading.

Assuming that you have taken responsibility for your feelings, then Principles 2 to 5 outline what attitudes you need to take towards life's adversities to enable you to respond healthily to them. These attitudes are the foundation of good mental health.

Of the four attitudes that I will discuss in Principles 2 to 5, Albert Ellis held that what I call in this book *flexible attitudes* are perhaps the most important – and I tend to agree with him. As I will show more fully in Principle 2 when you hold a flexible attitude towards an adversity you acknowledge that you desire that the adversity does not happen, but you also hold that your desire does not have to met. This attitude first allows you to be honest with yourself concerning what you want to happen in life and what you don't want to happen. It also enables you to devote your energy to dealing with the adversity rather than complaining internally (and perhaps even externally) about its existence.

Suppose you hold a flexible attitude towards an adversity. In that case, you will also tend to hold one or more of the following attitudes towards that adversity, attitudes that Ellis argued stem from your flexible attitude:

- A non-awfulising attitude (see Principle 3), where you hold that it is bad, but not terrible if the adversity happens;
- A discomfort tolerance attitude (see Principle 4), where you hold that while it is a struggle for you to tolerate the adversity at hand, you can tolerate it, it's worth tolerating, you are willing to tolerate it, and you are going to do so; and
- An unconditional acceptance towards the self, others and life conditions (see Principle 5) where you accept yourself unconditionally if you hold yourself responsible for the adversity, where you accept others unconditionally if you hold them responsible for the adversity and where you accept life conditions unconditionally if you hold these conditions responsible for the adversity.

In Principle 6, I discuss the view that good mental health is not associated with you experiencing positive feelings in the presence of life's adversities or even the absence of negative feelings in their presence. Rather, good mental health is associated with you experiencing healthy negative emotions (as opposed to unhealthy negative emotions) in the presence of these adversities. To illustrate my point, I discuss the following healthy negative emotions and contrast them with their unhealthy counterparts:

- Concern as opposed to anxiety;
- Sadness as opposed to depression;
- Healthy anger as opposed to unhealthy anger;
- Remorse as opposed to guilt; and
- Sorrow as opposed to hurt and self-pity.

Finally, in Principle 7 I briefly outline a realistic perspective on personal change, which presents several steps that you need to take if you are to achieve good mental health.

I hope you find this short book of use to you and I would appreciate any feedback that you may wish to give me sent to <u>windy@windydryden.com</u>

Windy Dryden
January 2021

PRINCIPLE 1

Take Personal Responsibility

Personal responsibility is an essential characteristic of mental well-being. I believe that circumstances within your sphere of influence are your responsibility. Consider for a moment the areas on which you have an impact. The principal matters that you can shape are those pertaining to you as an individual: your thoughts, attitudes, and feelings; your decisions and actions. Furthermore, you have some impact on the effect of your actions.

Absolute mastery of these concepts is impossible, however, as demonstrated by the following test on thought control. Close your eyes and imagine a white bear. After a moment, instruct yourself to stop imagining the white bear. Curiously, you will be unable to eliminate the thought of the white bear. Yet, if you accept the thought of the white bear, you will quickly tire of it and find you will think about other matters. This is an example of how you have some influence over your thoughts, despite not being able to master them completely. You alone are responsible for your thoughts, since they are generally within your sphere of influence. Although I suggested you try to think of a white bear, you alone are responsible for thinking of it, just as I am responsible for making the suggestion, since that is within my sphere of influence.

Your attitudes towards yourself, others and your life circumstances largely influence your feelings. As a consequence of being primarily responsible for these attitudes, you are responsible for the resulting emotions and feelings you encounter. However, an individual cannot have complete control over their attitudes and emotions since external events and conditions will also influence them.

To illustrate this point, consider a situation whereby you are unexpectedly made redundant from a job you have held for many years. This places you in adverse circumstances, which will influence your thoughts since you have lost a position which provided you with meaning, happiness and financial security. In these difficult circumstances, it is improbable that you will think, 'I'm pleased that I no longer have to work' or 'It does not matter to me that I have been made redundant.' In fact, these attitudes would be detrimental to you. Despite these adverse conditions, you would remain responsible for how you frame your predicament. You have the option of thinking in what I call a healthy negative manner, such as, 'I don't like being in this situation, but I can tolerate it', or in a disturbed negative manner, such as, 'I can't bear losing my job; my life is over.'

Circumstances and happenings in your life—especially those of a negative nature—will limit the types of attitudes you may have; however, they seldom *cause* the nature of your attitudes and feelings. Invariably, you still have the option to think in a healthy negative manner or a disturbed negative manner.

Additionally, individuals are primarily respons-ible for their choices, despite all the pertinent details not necessarily being available when that choice is made. For instance, let's assume that you are considering moving house since you do not get along with your neighbours who have recently moved in. You have three options to consider. You could move to house A. Alternatively, you could move to house B. On the other hand, you could decide to remain in your current property and continue your property search. (This choice risks the possibility that you may not find a property you desire or that the hunt may be lengthy.) You are responsible for researching each property and its area as thoroughly as possible and also for asking estate agents about the likelihood of a suitable property becoming available within an acceptable timeframe if you decide to remain in your current abode. Imagine you choose to move to property A. Unfortunately, it soon becomes apparent that several pertinent details were concealed, which would have resulted in you taking an alternative option had these details been made available to you. The responsibility for the choice remains yours, but you are not responsible for the fact that important information was concealed from you. In reality, it would be futile to demand that you absolutely should have been made aware of the details when the fact remains that you were not. Essentially, you are not responsible for knowing what you did not know. However, it is crucial that you take responsibility for assimilating knowledge from the event and applying this to similar events that may arise in the future; for instance, you could ask additional questions during a property search that you did not ask last time.

Further, you are responsible to an extent for the probable effects of your actions. To illustrate, let's suppose you have offered to swap shifts with a colleague to enable them to attend a function.

However, at the last moment, you change your mind and decide you would prefer not to work that particular shift. Your colleague considers that you have let him down and gets himself into a rage. What are you responsible for, and what are you not responsible for? In my view, you are responsible for not swapping shifts with him (your action), and since you knew that attending the function was important to him, you can take responsibility for him feeling displeased since he is hardly likely to be pleased or indifferent about your decision. However, your colleague's feelings of rage stem from his rigid attitude towards your decision and you are not responsible for his rigidity. He is!

Fundamentally, it is crucial that individuals take responsibility for their thoughts, feelings, decisions, actions and the probable effects of these actions. Accepting personal responsibility empowers you to endeavour to make changes where possible; if you do not accept responsibility, you are likely to instead blame others or circumstances for your attitudes, feelings, decisions and actions. Blaming others and external events instead of taking responsibility is a crucial indicator of poor mental health. Using blame instead of taking responsibility indicates that you perceive yourself as a victim and the world through a lens of weakness and vulnerability. Suppose you think you are unable to assume personal responsibility. In that case, you also deny having any control of your life, leading you to feel it necessary to be saved by others and becoming reliant on them. When you see yourself as a victim, you think that life has dealt you an unjust hand and that you have been ill-treated by other people and by life. You deny that you have played any part in these things happening to you when the truth is that you probably have.

This means you will be inclined to blame your upbringing and background for your current attitudes, feelings and actions. Regrettably, this is encouraged by some psychological perspectives, since there is no clear differentiation between incidents *contributing* to attitudes, feelings and actions, and *causing* them. I believe that these incidents impact, but seldom give rise to, your actions today. Your attitudes towards experiences are the principal drivers of your reactions today. For instance, your parents may have indoctrinated you in the attitude that making a mistake means you are worthless. Subsequently, you have likely cultivated this attitude in your mind for as long as you can remember, which, in my opinion, means you are responsible for persevering with this attitude. You can alter it.

Responsibility and Blame

There is a crucial difference between responsibility and blame. Although I believe that individuals should accept responsibility for their attitudes, feelings, decisions and actions, I do not mean that they should be blamed for these attitudes, etc. Blame suggests that people are bad if they do something inadequate or unacceptable and should be punished accordingly. Throughout this book, my perspective is that we are all imperfect and prone to making errors, but we are neither good nor bad. It follows, then, that blame is unnecessary: it is taking responsibility that is important. In my opinion, you will be unable to gain knowledge from your mistakes if you blame yourself, since if you are to blame, you must be a bad person, and will continue to be so, rather than to use new knowledge to effect change.

Summary

In summary, accept personal responsibility for what you can have an impact on: your attitudes, feelings, decisions, and actions. Consequently, you will be empowered to reshape harmful thought patterns associated with problematic or troubling emotions and behaviours. If you acknowledge personal responsibility, you will reap the rewards of the rest of this book. Otherwise, if you continue to absolve yourself of personal responsibility, it is improbable that this book—or any other—will facilitate any change or success.

*

In the next principle, I will discuss why it is important to keep your attitude towards life's adversities flexible.

PRINCIPLE 2

Keep Your Attitudes Flexible

In Principle 1, I outlined how your feelings and actions are shaped mainly by the attitudes you possess regarding life experiences. Consequently, to enjoy mental well-being, it is necessary to alter and expand the array of attitudes you hold so that they are conducive to doing so.

A Framework for Human Emotions

How do we differentiate between a flexible attitude which is associated with good mental health outcomes and an inflexible attitude, which is associated with poor mental health outcomes? I frequently guide my clients through a framework for human emotions to help them answer this question and will use this framework here. The framework comprises three parts.

Part 1

I would like you to contemplate that you think it to be preferable and advisable to always have at least sixteen pounds with you. It is not that you consider this to be absolutely necessary, just favourable. Now contemplate looking into your wallet to assess how much money you have with you, whilst possessing this attitude, and realising that you have only fifteen pounds on your person. Since you always prefer— not demand—to carry sixteen pounds with you, imagine how you may feel to discover you have only fifteen pounds. You may imagine yourself feeling concerned, annoyed or displeased. In my opinion, these are healthy negative emotions, since they empower you to adapt to these unfavourable circumstances and prompt you to take remedial steps if necessary.

Part 2

I would like you to contemplate this time that your attitude is that it is not simply preferable, but it is absolutely imperative to always have at least sixteen pounds with you, and it would be terrible if you did not. Considering this attitude, imagine how you may feel to discover you have only fifteen pounds. You will likely discern that you would feel a completely different array of negative—and unhealthy—emotions: anxiety, unhealthy anger or depression perhaps? It is improbable that these emotions would empower you to adapt to the circumstances or prompt you to take action to rectify the situation.

Bear in mind that in parts 1 and 2 of the framework, the situation you confront—having fifteen pounds in your wallet—and your preferences are identical. Nevertheless, the disparate negative feelings you experience—first of all, healthy and subsequently unhealthy—are rooted in different attitudes. During the first part, you maintained a flexible attitude, and in the second part, your attitude became rigid.

Part 3

For the concluding part of the framework, I would like you to consider that your attitude is the same rigid attitude you contemplated in Part 2—that it is not simply preferable, but absolutely crucial that you always have at least sixteen pounds with you. It would be the end of the world if you did not. Consider how you may feel if you discover three-pound coins upon frantically looking through your wallet of which you were previously unaware. The majority of people would report feeling reassured or relieved, which is likely at first, given you are now in possession of more than your absolute minimum of sixteen pounds. Yet, since you hold a rigid attitude of 'It is not simply preferable, but absolutely crucial that I always have at least sixteen pounds with me, and it would be the end of the world if I did not', you would become aware of a notion that would result in feelings of unhealthy distress and fear once more. You may begin to deliberate in such a manner as, 'What if I need to pay out three pounds? What if I lose three pounds? What if someone steals from me?' Despite having more than your absolute minimum, you once more feel overwhelmed by anxiety and unhealthy distress.

The crux of this framework—which is central to an understanding of emotional disturbance and health—is this. Everybody—whatever age, gender, ethnicity or socioeconomic status—feels emotionally disturbed when they do not possess what they think it is essential to have and is susceptible to feeling disturbed when they do possess such things in case they cease to retain them. Nonetheless, suppose we adhere closely (not rigidly!) to our flexible attitudes. In that case, we will still experience negative feelings if we do not possess what we desire, but which it is not crucial for us to have. However, these negative feelings will be healthy and empower us to adapt to the circumstances and take remedial measures to effect change.

The Advantages of Flexible Attitudes

Individuals live their lives in keeping with an intricate array of aspirations. There are circumstances that you yearn for and others that you would prefer do not occur. Individuals desire particular things from others and possess a healthy range of preferences regarding their environment and circumstances. The framework illustrated above demonstrates how you can experience emotional well-being despite not achieving what you desire, as long as you maintain a flexible attitude—in other words, if you adhere to your desires, but do not demand that they are fulfilled. In Principle 6, I will discuss how particular negative feelings demonstrate a healthy response to circumstances in which you do not achieve your aspirations. A flexible attitude of aspirations and desires that are non-essential empowers you to adapt to circumstances that you cannot modify and encourages you to make alterations to effect change where possible, in the absence of feelings of emotional disturbance. Also, a flexible attitude will prompt you to take an approach to achieve what you desire. Accordingly, a flexible attitude of non-essential preferences and aspirations motivates you to achieve life satisfaction.

The Disadvantages of Rigid Attitudes

Conversely, rigid attitudes comprise preferences and aspirations that you make absolutely crucial and indispensable in your mind, giving rise to two eventualities. In the first instance, emotional disturbance becomes more probable when you transform your desires into absolutely crucial and indispensable needs and these 'needs' are not achieved. Also, your propensity to emotional disturbance intensifies even though you have that which you consider essential, because you are aware that you can lose what you 'need'. Second, a rigid attitude generates behaviours that make it less likely that you will achieve your aspirations. As exemplified in the framework above, a rigid attitude engenders anxiety, and if you feel anxious, it is improbable that your actions will be productive.

Anxiety makes you feel that you are trying to juggle ten balls all at once, causing you to blunder around frantically in an attempt to keep anything from hitting the floor. Do you consider this a useful framework to inspire you to be effective? Certainly not! Yet, transposing your rigid attitudes, which cultivate your anxious feelings, into flexible attitudes produces healthy negative emotions, such as concern and disappointment. These healthy negative feelings have the purpose of prompting you to realise your circumstances' true nature and consider action to reshape them if this is feasible.

The 'BUT' in Flexible Attitudes and the 'AND THEREFORE' in Rigid Attitudes

Each individual will have their unique aspirations; for instance, you may wish to own your own home or get married; you may wish to learn a new skill or live a healthier lifestyle. Each of these represents a healthy aspiration, providing that the word BUT follows them. Therefore, if you wish to get married, a beneficial statement would be: 'I would like to get married, BUT I do not have to.' If you want to learn a new skill, a healthy attitude would be: 'I would like to learn this new skill and will make my best effort, BUT I do not need to learn it.'

The action of removing the BUT from your attitudes means that you can always transform your flexible aspirations into rigid fundamentals with the addition of the phrase AND THEREFORE. Thus: 'I would like to get married AND THEREFORE I must do so' or 'I would like to learn this new skill, and I will make my best effort, AND THEREFORE I do need to learn it.' A rigid attitude is central to emotional disturbance and creates a susceptibility to it, regardless of what you consider essential.

To achieve mental well-being, it is necessary to consider your aspirations, endeavour to fulfil them and resolve difficulties that may arise in striving to achieve them. Furthermore, you will maintain mental well-being if you desist from changing your aspirations into rigid fundamentals. Yet, if you permit this change to transpire, the consequence will be poor mental health.

The Difficulties with Rigid Attitudes

There are three difficulties with rigid attitudes.

1. As the framework illustrates, if you maintain a rigid attitude, your aspirations become essential, which induces poor emotional well-being and behavioural problems.

2. Rigid attitudes are incompatible with real life. Since there is no law declaring that you must possess whatever you desire, rigid attitudes are not in accordance with reality.

3. Those who possess a rigid attitude become aware of their aspirations and stipulate that these must be fulfilled. However, logically, an aspiration cannot lead to a demand. For instance, consider this question: Would you like two thousand pounds to be paid into your bank account instantly? Your answer is likely to be 'Yes'. Nevertheless, is it sensible to consider that simply because you desire this money, it definitely must be paid into your account right now? Clearly not! Accordingly, rigid attitudes are illogical since aspirations do not logically lead to demands that one's aspirations must be met.

*

In this principle, I made the case for adopting a flexible attitude towards life's adversities and discussed the difficulties with holding a rigid attitude. In the following principle, I will discuss the importance of accepting but not liking reality when it is negative. I will also explain why it is important to avoid an attitude called 'awfulising' while striving to accept reality.

PRINCIPLE 3

Accept Reality and Avoid 'Awfulising'

What Does 'Accepting Reality' Signify?

In endeavouring to achieve mental well-being, it is important to establish an attitude that accepts real life. This is commonly misconstrued as a suggestion that individuals should resign themselves to reality, which is entirely untrue. Resignation may imply that one has very little or no power to effect any change. Consequently, being resigned to circumstances precludes any attempt to modify them and so the circumstances remain the same. For that reason, I am not suggesting that you should resign yourself to unfavourable circumstances or that you should not take practical steps to effect change. Not for a moment. In accepting reality, individuals recognise that the prevailing circumstances have arisen since all the requisite factors exist for them to do so. Also, they realise that they can take practical steps to modify these factors, which generates a change in circumstances.

Accepting reality is sometimes misinterpreted as a suggestion to either appreciate reality or become uninterested in it; once more, this is far from the truth. To illustrate, I would like you to imagine that you have applied for a training course which you are eager to take up, but you are not successful. In suggesting that you accept the reality of this situation, I would not be implying that you should be happy that your application was unsuccessful. This would not be realistic, since it would be necessary for you to be of the unusual opinion that, 'I am happy that my application has been rejected for a training course I wanted to take up.' I would also not suggest that you should be uninterested in the application being unsuccessful, since this would result in the most extraordinary resignation, and would require you to think that, 'I am unconcerned as to whether my application is successful or not.' This would be untrue!

In this instance, accepting reality signifies that:

- You concede that your application has been rejected, although you are unsure why at present;
- You are disappointed because it is contradictory to your aspirations; and

- You contemplate requesting reconsideration of your application.

Regarding the latter point, you may make enquiries to determine the reason that your application was rejected. If you then conclude that the explanation is unjust, you may request reconsideration of your application. In this way, you are attempting to alter the factors that existed and contributed to your application being unsuccessful. Yet, this attempt to change those factors may not necessarily be successful. It is probable that you may not be provided with details of the reason for your application being rejected or that your request for reconsideration—should you make one—is also rejected.

Therefore, accepting reality comprises three important points:

- You acknowledge that the circumstances have arisen and that all the necessary factors are in situ for them to do so;
- You acknowledge that the circumstances are contradictory to your aspirations and you are unhappy about them; and
- You contemplate taking practical steps to attempt to modify the circumstances.

Further, if you are unsuccessful in your endeavours to alter the circumstances, in order to accept reality, you would be required to concede that your initiatives failed and that this is also regrettable.

The Meaning of 'Awfulising'

Individuals each hold numerous aspirations of variable intensity. On the whole, the more sincere the aspiration, the more negative your feelings will be if your aspiration is not accomplished. Failure to attain these sincere aspirations may make it challenging to abide by the three points above, and it may be easier to partake in the process of 'awfulising'.

An awfulising attitude constitutes (1) you being accurately aware that it is disagreeable that you have not satisfied your aspiration; (2) you rigidly insisting that these circumstances unequivocally should not have arisen; and (3) you deducing that since that which unequivocally should not have occurred has done so, it is not simply disagreeable, it is horrible, terrible and the end of the world.

Almost without exception, this awfulising attitude is a tremendously overstated pessimistic judgment. Although you may initially judge un-pleasant situations on a scale of 0–99.9 per cent in terms of how disagreeable they are, you may then contrive an entirely individual scale of terror with a rating from 101 per cent disagreeable to infinity. The outcome of maintaining an awfulising attitude is that at that juncture, you consider that nothing could be worse. If you briefly consider this notion, its absurdity is swiftly revealed. It is undeniable that the situation is being blown completely out of proportion.

How to Modify an Awfulising Attitude

To alter your awfulising attitude, you should examine its constituent parts.

First, consider what evidence supports your attitude that these disagreeable circumstances absolutely should not have arisen. You will likely reach the understanding that these events occur since all the requisite factors for their existence are present. Therefore, it would be nonsensical and unrealistic to insist that these circumstances absolutely should not exist—that reality must not be reality. It is comparable to rigidly insisting that when one atom of carbon and two atoms of oxygen combine, it absolutely should not produce carbon dioxide. Considering that all the essential factors exist for carbon dioxide production—carbon and oxygen—it is clear that this is what will result. If you demand that carbon and oxygen should not produce carbon dioxide, it will not prevent this eventuality in these circumstances. Therefore, rigidly insisting that an event, such as your application being rejected, should not have occurred will not give rise to it being accepted. The greater your insistence that the event absolutely should not have transpired, the more considerable your emotional disturbance. Should you resolve to initiate an appeal in this state of mind, your emotional state will probably aggravate the situation and be detrimental to your success.

Next, you should examine the notion that the disagreeable circumstances exceed 100 per cent on your scale of unpleasantness. Dr Albert Ellis, who founded Rational Emotive Behaviour Therapy in 1955, was speaking to an audience regarding awfulising attitudes and stated that there could be nothing worse than being run over by a steam-roller—this would be 100 per cent disagreeable. However, a person in the audience disputed this by saying, 'Dr Ellis, even being run over by a steamroller is not 100 per cent bad because you could be run over by that steamroller more slowly!'

Dr Miller's Rating Scale

My American associate, Dr Tom Miller, uses an original technique to help people reconsider an awfulising attitude. He would ask you to assume that having all four of your limbs severed would be 100 per cent bad. Subsequently, you would be requested to rate ever lesser events; for example, having three limbs severed (perhaps 90 per cent bad); having two limbs severed (maybe 80 per cent bad); having one limb severed (perhaps 70 per cent bad); and so forth, down to having a finger severed (perhaps 10 per cent bad) or a permanent scar on your face (maybe 5 per cent bad). After that, Dr Miller would enquire if your application being turned down was as disagreeable as having all four of your limbs severed. Was it as unpleasant as having three limbs severed? What about one limb? In applying his method in my practice with numerous clients, hardly anyone would rate their application being rejected as worse than sustaining a permanent scar to their face. This process may appear unusual, but it is striking and powerful enough to help gain a sense of perspective and proportion.

I trust that you will realise that when you assess a situation as awful, you are forming a tremendously overstated negative judgment of a situation which is undeniably unpleasant. However, it is far from as unpleasant as you deem it under the influence of your awfulising attitude.

When Tragedies Occur, Do Not Affix an Awfulising Attitude

There are adverse situations which would attain a very high rating on any scale of adversity. Individuals suffer tragedies—bereavements, serious accidents or injuries, and experience disasters, such as a major flood or fire. The tragic nature of these events should not be trivialised. Unfortunately, no matter how much we may desire to live in the absence of these tragic events, they will endure. In this context, accepting reality suggests that: (a) tragedies may occur in your life; (b) you cannot be spared or exempted from tragedy, nor do you have to be; and (c) tragedies are very bad and may have long-lasting implications.

Nevertheless, applying an awfulising attitude to a tragedy fundamentally stipulates that the tragedy *must* not materialise in your life. Since a statute of exemption does not protect you, you are not immune from personal tragedy. Therefore, if you suffer tragedy, it is vital not to affix emotional disturbance to the already heavy burden of sadness, which is a healthy reaction. This is not to suggest that the highly disruptive nature of any tragedy should be trivialised, but to urge you to accept the fact that reality can be tragic and to desist from affixing an awfulising attitude to tragedies.

When Unfairness Occurs, Do Not Affix an Awfulising Attitude

As outlined, tragedies do, unfortunately, occur in life. Furthermore, unfairness also happens in life, and you may be subject to unfairness, no matter how unwarranted this may be—again, you are not exempt from unfairness, nor do you need to be. To accept the reality of inequity, you are required to: (a) relinquish your insistence that since you are undeserving of unfair conduct, it absolutely should not occur; (b) concede that the factors that precipitated the unfairness were in place and so, theoretically, the outcome is to be anticipated, just as carbon and oxygen combined make carbon dioxide; (c) assess the injustice on a realistic scale of badness, considering and in proportion to the ratings already ascribed to the various tragedies above; and (d) take remedial steps to effect change if possible or accept but not like it if it is not.

Accepting Change and Uncertainty

You will be familiar with the adage that change happens continuously in this world; in fact, you are experiencing change and shift as you read this. Other people are perpetually evolving too, as are relationships with those around you. If you insist that there must be no transformation or evolution of you, others or life and that they continue to be the same, you are maintaining an attitude which does not accept reality. Change will transpire regardless and will not be affected by you maintaining this attitude and insisting that life must continue to be the same. Therefore, wouldn't accepting this without disturbing yourself about it effect better mental well-being? This is helpfully illustrated by King Canute's story, who perceived himself as omnipotent and consequently confronted the rising tide and ordered it to retreat. Do you remember the outcome? The tide advanced regardless of King Canute's demands for it to withdraw and he got wet feet!

Spurning the notion of accepting reality and instead insisting that certainty must prevail in your life would be detrimental to your mental well-being. This is the case because the one sure thing is that there is no certainty in life, since transition and shift occur, frequently in an unforeseen fashion. As a result, no amount of dogmatic insistence on your part will generate the certainty you desire in your life. If you rigidly insist on certainty in your life, you will continue to experience uncertainty, yet you will also experience emotional disturbance. To achieve good mental health, it is vital to relinquish your insistence that life must be certain and, despite your healthy preference for certainty, accept the uncertain nature of the world.

Do Not Emulate Procrustes

You may desire life experiences to be specific and unambiguous, and as a result, you will classify matters into two sets—black or white. Regrettably, life is far from so well defined. The intricate essence of the world and life situations makes it incapable of being arranged into two distinct sets. Consider Procrustes' actions in attempting to do so. Procrustes owned a hostel where he offered a bed for the night to passing travellers. For his visitors to have a comfortable night's sleep, he was convinced that they must fit the bed precisely; hence, he would sever the legs of those who were too tall and stretch the legs of those who were too short. If you insist that things must be specific and explicit, you adopt a similar mindset to Procrustes. You will endure hardship through emotional disturbance, and your insistence will have no bearing on the ambiguities of life.

Accept Pluralism and Non-Utopianism

Your mental well-being is also negatively affected by an additional non-accepting attitude you may maintain—the dogmatic insistence that you are right. Individuals who demand that they are right are convinced that they hold the correct opinions and know the best way to do things and that others are wrong if they adopt a different perspective. This attitude is frequently the basis of conflict, as demonstrated in Edward de Bono's book *I Am Right, You Are Wrong*. If you hold this attitude, you find it intolerable if others oppose or dispute your opinions and you can't acknowledge that other, contrasting, valid viewpoints exist. This unyielding rigid attitude is at the core of extremism and terrorism.

Realistically, human existence cannot be organised into distinct groups of correct or incorrect, since each argument can be viewed from numerous perspectives. Every situation can be considered from disparate, but similarly plausible, standpoints. Therefore, pluralism is prevalent, and universally-held viewpoints rarely exist in any area of human enterprise. It is important to recognise that you hold a specific opinion, which you feel is correct, but that others maintain contrasting perspectives, which they are permitted to do—in this way you are acknowledging the existence of pluralism. If extremists and terrorists could only accept this, the world would be considerably safer.

Lastly, to accept reality, it is important that you assume a non-utopian viewpoint, where you appreciate that the nature of existence can be both positive and negative. This is not to suggest that you assume an excessively gullible cheerfulness in the style of Pollyanna, where you suppose that the future will be rosy with no difficulties. I am also not suggesting that you assume an excessively defeatist viewpoint, where you presume that the future will be bleak with nothing promising to anticipate. A non-utopian ideology emphasises maximising the favourable features of life, whilst also acknowledging and minimising unfavourable features. Ultimately, this philosophy concedes that reality comprises an assortment of agreeable and disagreeable features, rather than being exclusively agreeable or disagreeable.

*

In this principle, I have explained why adopting an attitude of acceptance of reality is conducive to good mental health. When facing life's adversities, it is not only important that you accept this reality, but that you respond healthily to the discomfort that you will inevitably feel when you do not get your desires met. When this happens, it is important for you to adopt an attitude of discomfort tolerance and in the next principle, I will outline the five components of this attitude and show you how to develop it.

PRINCIPLE 4

Adopt an Attitude of Discomfort Tolerance

Introduction

Individuals continually encounter choices which have ramifications on their life in the short and long term. If in this situation, you have an option that will help you attain both your short-term and your long-term objectives, your decision-making process will generally be straightforward. However, complications arise if your short-term goals are incompatible with your long-term goals. In my opinion, to enjoy mental well-being, it is important that you endeavour to attain equilibrium between your short- and long-term objectives. In persistently delaying attempts to attain your short-term goals while striving for your long-term goals, life may become quite unfulfilling. Nevertheless, relentlessly pursuing your short-term objectives and disregarding your long-term objectives may provide some initial enjoyment, but you may find that existence seems superficial and dull. If you seek to achieve equilibrium in pursuit of your short- and long-term objectives, you will feel both a sense of instant satisfaction, and that you are striving towards purposeful goals.

Based on forty-five years of counselling experience, I have found that individuals seem to find it especially arduous to tolerate short-term hardship in pursuit of their long-term ambitions. Why is it so problematic to surrender instant satisfaction when this conduct would ultimately produce far greater fulfilment and accomplishment? This is primarily due to us habitually heeding an attitude of discomfort intolerance. If you maintain an attitude of discomfort intolerance, you may:

- Often postpone taking action;
- Maintain a disorderly way of life;
- Customarily fail to persist with endeavours that would have been to your benefit; and
- Be at pains to steer clear of difficult situations, regardless of the reality that managing these difficulties would enable you to become more capable and resourceful. For example, you may avoid dealing with your

financial records, thinking that ignorance is bliss.

Furthermore, maintaining an attitude of discomfort intolerance may cause you to remedy issues in a cursory manner; therefore, you may be a heavy smoker, a compulsive eater or spender, or consume too much alcohol.

If this sounds familiar, you are probably caught in the 'comfort trap' and doubtless maintain an attitude of discomfort intolerance.

Principal Examples of the Discomfort Intolerance Attitude

Here are several principal examples of a discomfort intolerance attitude.

'I must not be frustrated'

The first problematic attitude is the notion that you unreservedly should not feel frustrated, and if you do, that is horrifying, and you are unable to endure it. In respect of frustration, I refer to your journey in pursuit of your aspirations being obstructed. If you maintain this attitude and experience frustration, you will operate with the sole conviction that you must eliminate it as swiftly as possible, regardless of future ramifications. Since your solitary consideration is to eliminate frustration *now*, you disregard any future implications.

'I must be comfortable now'

Connected to the first attitude, the second discomfort intolerance attitude is that you must find your current situation agreeable. If you find it disagreeable, that would be intolerable. If you attain an agreeable situation, you may struggle to keep it. If so, your demand for comfort will lead you to be unwilling to suffer a brief period of discomfort, even though doing so may provide considerable benefits to you.

Let's suppose that you are resting comfortably in bed and you are aware that you need to complete a shopping trip. If you hold that you must be comfortable in the moment, it will probably require a tremendous incentive for you to get up; therefore, you will only do so when not completing the shopping trip becomes more disagreeable. You maintain the ideology that you must be comfortable in the moment; however, completing the shopping trip at some point becomes more agreeable than not doing so. Insisting on an agreeable situation will prompt you always to select the most agreeable course of action, even though doing so may have negative implications in the future.

'I must not experience negative feelings'

Maintaining that you must not encounter negative feelings and that this would be intolerable, makes it probable that two things will occur. First, you will be at pains to steer clear of experiences that you anticipate may prompt negative feelings, despite these feelings potentially being a healthy response and that facing them may give rise to significant fulfilment. Your life will be extremely limited since the concept of avoidance will control it. You may feel that you would not need to avoid situations if the world were more pleasant and people were kinder. In light of your avoidance of experiences that may prompt negative feelings, you avoid taking healthy risks, with the result that you overestimate negativity. At no point do you consider that you could survive any negative experiences that you face—your solitary regard is to avoid negative feelings.

Second, suppose you maintain a discomfort intolerance attitude regarding negative feelings and it becomes inevitable that you must confront them.

In that case, the intensity of your negative emotions may be magnified. This is frequently obvious in terms of experiences of anxiety. You may believe that you must not feel anxious, and if you did, it would be dreadful and you would be unable to tolerate it. Therefore, you feel 'anxiety about anxiety', which you may accelerate into an acute panic.

These two demonstrations of your attitude that you must not experience negative feelings tend to coexist. As a result, you maintain the concept of avoidance at the core of your existence; however, you will accelerate your anxiety into an acute panic since it is impossible to eliminate negativity.

'I must experience pleasant feelings'

Suppose you maintain a discomfort intolerance attitude that you must experience pleasant feelings. In that case, you will deem it essential that you always experience feelings of contentment and satisfaction and that it would be awful if you didn't. Consequently, you will experience one of a variety of troublesome sequences of events. You may develop an addiction and endeavour to achieve a pleasant feeling by smoking, consuming alcohol or food, or taking drugs such as marijuana, cocaine or heroin. You may develop a behavioural addiction, such as to gambling or exercise. The difficulty is that since the pleasurable feelings that result from addictions are only short-lived, you will soon experience a powerful urge to consume the substance or perform the activity again. If you do this over time, you will eventually get into a lot of trouble as you maintain your addiction unchecked.

If you maintain that you must always feel contented, you may assume a safer lifestyle; however, you may experience perpetual apathy in doing so. This attitude also gives rise to you paying increased attention to negative elements of every activity, even those you deem to be pleasurable. For instance, Ben, who maintains that he must always feel happy, is a keen squash player. Ben is eager before his squash game since he holds a misconception that the event will be entirely agreeable. However, there are some elements of exasperation inherent in any sport, on which he quickly begins to focus. If his opponent is not challenging enough, he will feel bored, whereas if his opponent is far superior, he will feel disheartened. Also, he becomes exasperated with the need to gather balls from around the court and if the other player passes the ball to him imprecisely on switching server. Individuals like Ben will never feel contented, because every situation, no matter how enjoyable, encompasses some aggravating elements. As a consequence of their attitude, the Bens of this world concentrate on these negative elements, insist that they should not exist, overestimate them in their mind and therefore deprive themselves of contentment.

Procrastination

It is clear from the discussion of the four attitudes above—I must not be frustrated; I must be comfortable; I must not experience negative feelings; I must experience pleasant feelings—that if you hold these attitudes, you will be liable to procrastination. The word derives from the Latin words for 'forward' and 'of tomorrow', which suggests you are prone to postponing that which would be better done today. You will formulate what you regard as persuasive arguments for delaying action that it is vital to take today. In truth, these 'arguments' are just justifications or excuses, which may comprise the following:

1. *I must be in the right frame of mind to begin this task.* This is incorrect since we regularly begin tasks when we are not inclined to do so, but

then adopt a more motivated disposition due to pursuing the activity!

2. *I need the comfort of a deadline to motivate me to complete this task. I can't bear the discomfort of starting a task when I don't need to.* This is also incorrect. You may only work when you have the pressure of a deadline if you are prone to procrastination since you will delay tasks until it becomes more disagreeable to procrastinate than to begin the task. Nevertheless, this pressure is not essential for you to start the task. You can start it earlier even if you are making yourself move from the comfort of what you are doing to the discomfort of doing the task. Doing so means that you complete the task earlier and in so doing, you have taught yourself that you don't need a deadline to motivate you.

You may procrastinate because it has an inbuilt excuse that you can employ; for example, if you allow inadequate time to finish a piece of work and your output is substandard, you can excuse it as a consequence of a lack of time. This absolves you from acknowledging that you may need to enhance your capabilities or knowledge. Unfortunately, shielding yourself from this critical knowledge of your weaknesses by justifying your actions leads to your learning little from these experiences.

Establishing a Flexible Attitude to Enable Discomfort Tolerance

How can you establish an attitude of discomfort tolerance to enjoy better mental well-being? In doing so, you need to scrutinise and deconstruct the rigid concepts at the core of the attitude of discomfort intolerance. Therefore, it is important to become attuned to yourself avoiding feelings of exasperation or negative situations, pursuing satisfaction or contentment, or partaking in activities that are to your detriment to achieve short-term fulfilment. Subsequently, it would help if you examined the following kinds of attitudes:

- 'I must not be frustrated';
- 'I must be comfortable';
- 'I must not experience negative feelings'; and
- 'I must experience pleasant feelings.'

In scrutinising these attitudes, it is necessary to consider three questions. Primarily, and fundamentally, 'Is this attitude engendering a successful life and mental well-being, or does it create adversity for me and conflict with others and obstruct the achievement of my long-term aspirations?' Undoubtedly, concepts that derive from an attitude of discomfort intolerance create long-term difficulties.

The second question you need to consider is, 'Have any universal rules or regulations been established that absolve me from experiencing frustration, disagreeable situations and negativity or that stipulate that circumstances must contrive to be agreeable for me?' These universal rules and regulations are imaginary; the world does not observe them. If it did, you would always be absolved from feelings of frustration, unpleasant situations and negativity. You would continually experience agreeable circumstances and, further, there would be no negative repercussions in the future. Regrettably, the world is not governed by what you command, and if you continue to assume that your demanding attitudes should be fulfilled, you will persist in defeating yourself. Indeed, continue to pursue your aspirations, such as minimising frustration and negativity and healthily seeking contentment but, essentially, strive to achieve a healthy equilibrium between attaining your short- and long-term objectives.

Lastly, consider the question, 'Since I desire not to experience frustration, would it be reasonable to infer that I must never experience frustration?' This is not a well-reasoned argument: wanting something not to happen does not logically denote that it must.

It is important that you examine and dismantle these ideas regularly and, most importantly, you need to act on your new healthy, flexible attitudes. Thus, while examining the idea that you must not be frustrated, it is important that you act according to the idea that frustration is undesirable but that it is necessary to put up with it if you are to achieve more meaningful goals. There is no law which states that you must not be frustrated. Frustration is a fact of life. Developing this attitude will help you to problem-solve your way out of the frustration situation if this is possible.

Developing an attitude of discomfort tolerance involves a paradox. Changing your attitude of discomfort intolerance and acquiring an attitude of discomfort tolerance is frustrating and uncomfortable. But if you show yourself that it is worth tolerating and you resolve to act on this, regularly, you can do it.

Confronting the 'I Can't Stand It' Attitude

Another important concept to examine and adapt is the notion that you despise feeling frustrated, uncomfortable and negative, rather than content, and it is unendurable. The 'I can't stand it' attitude indicates two points: (1) if you do experience frustration, for instance, you will, without doubt, drop down dead; and (2) if there is frustration in the world and it cannot be eliminated, you will never feel content again. These would be exceptional circumstances! In reality, you can tolerate that which you hold you cannot endure.

It is necessary to consider the same three questions about the 'I can't stand it' attitude as you did for the 'demanding' attitude. First, if you think that you can't stand feeling uncomfortable, will this engender success and mental well-being or obstruct the achievement of your long-term aspirations? Almost invariably, it will be the latter. Second, have any rules or regulations been established that indicate that you can't stand being frustrated? Should these exist, you would be unable to bear it in even the most extreme of situations, such as saving a loved one's life. Framed in that manner, it is clear that the notion of frustration being in-tolerable, for instance, is entirely absurd. Lastly, consider whether, since it is onerous to bear feeling uncomfortable, it can be inferred that it is unimaginable that you could bear it? This is, once more, a significant oversimplification.

Develop the Five Components of a Discomfort Tolerance Attitude

I have examined discomfort tolerance attitudes quite closely and have concluded that any such attitude has the following five components:

1. **A struggle component.** Here, you acknowledge that it is often a struggle for you to tolerate discomfort. This is a fact and is true whether you end up by holding a discomfort tolerance attitude or a discomfort intolerance attitude.

2. **A discomfort tolerance component.** Even though tolerating discomfort is a struggle, you can tolerate it as this component makes clear.

3. **A 'worth it' component.** This component emphasises the point that while it may be possible for you to tolerate discomfort, there needs to be a purpose for you doing so, and if there isn't, you would be justified in not doing so. So, keep your mind on the intention of tolerating discomfort before making your decision to do so or not.

4. **A 'willingness' component.** You may see that there is a purpose for you to tolerate discomfort. Still, unless you are willing to go through the experience of tolerating it, then the purpose of doing so will become theoretical.

5. **A 'going to' component.** You may be willing to tolerate discomfort, but unless you will do so and act on this commitment, then willingness and the first three components will not lead to action.

Conclusion

It is vital for you to examine and deconstruct your discomfort intolerance notions and behave in accordance with your new discomfort tolerance notions in transposing your 'I can't stand it' attitude to one where you consider, 'This is unpleasant, but I can tolerate it.' Eventually, you will become more accustomed to these alternative thoughts, but in the meantime, you can refer to the five components of discomfort tolerance listed above as necessary.

Unfortunately, there has been limited focus on the attitude of discomfort tolerance in the study of mental health, despite it being of fundamental importance. Subsequently, I have examined it extensively here. For further information and details of techniques to develop an attitude of discomfort tolerance, please refer to my book, *How to Come Out of Your Comfort Zone* (Sheldon Press, 2012).

*

Perhaps the most important relationship you will have in this world is with yourself and so, in the following principle, I will show you what it takes to develop a healthy attitude towards yourself.

PRINCIPLE 5

Adopt a Healthy Attitude Towards Yourself

There is an abundance of books available to guide you in enhancing your relationships with other people. However, a much smaller number help you develop a more caring and more considerate relationship with yourself. Nevertheless, our relationship with ourselves often influences our relationships with other people and our environment. The prominent American psychologist, Albert Ellis, conjectured that if you are unable to live at peace with yourself, you cannot anticipate being able to do so with other people. Therefore, in this part of the book, I will discuss the salient features of a healthy attitude towards yourself.

Unconditional Self-Acceptance

An initial key feature entails you adopting a stance of unconditional acceptance of yourself. Unconventionally, I disagree with the idea of self-esteem; if you

define self-esteem carefully, I believe you will con-
cur. First, consider the definition of the self. I agree
with Dr Paul Hauck, my late friend and associate,
who suggested in his book *Hold Your Head Up High*
(Sheldon Press, 1992) that the self comprises our
attributes, attitudes, beliefs, feelings, actions, interests and other characteristics. Consequently, to
esteem your 'self' — which is defined as assigning an
overall grading to your 'self' — it is necessary to
know everything about yourself from the moment of
your birth until your death. It would be impossible to
acquire or document the billions of details derived
from the factors mentioned above.

Additionally, what impetus is there for assigning
yourself a universal grading? Is this to determine
whether you will be judged as fit for heaven? Its
purpose is not better mental well-being, because for
you to be a valuable individual, everything about
you would be required to be valuable. This is
unattainable, as we are all, essentially, flawed;
therefore, we are prone to making errors and are
formed of an intricate blend of positive, negative and
neutral factors.

A further point in my opposition to the idea of
self-esteem is due to it generally being conditional.
Therefore, you may deem yourself to be a valuable

(or more worthy) person assuming the presence of particular conditions, such as behaving capably, gaining the love of significant others, being moral and benevolent. If you deem that you are a valuable (or more worthy) person in the presence of particular conditions, should these evolve, you will be susceptible to feeling disturbed. Why? Because if behaving in a principled manner indicates that you are a valuable individual, you are, accordingly, less valuable should you behave less morally. This is an oversimplification since you are helpfully analysing your behaviour—for instance, 'I behaved in an unprincipled manner'—but then making an over-generalisation and an oversimplification by applying a universal grading to your entire self based on your behaviour. You are also categorising yourself in a manner that is not justified by one or a few actions.

Accepting an ideology of conditional self-esteem for behaving capably, for instance, will continue to generate feelings of anxiety, regardless of you deeming yourself a valuable individual since it is necessary for you to sustain your capable behaviour to preserve your value. On account of every individual being flawed, you will invariably make errors and behave less capably. Therefore, if your self-esteem is conditional on you demonstrating capable behaviour, you will remain susceptible to anxiety and other forms of emotional disturbance.

Healthy mental well-being and less emotional disturbance can be achieved by adopting one of two significant alternatives to conditional self-esteem. The first alternative is unconditional self-esteem. Although you continue to assert that you must assign yourself a universal grading—which, as we have examined, causes difficulties—you establish your self-esteem on conditions which will endure; for instance, you may deem yourself valuable purely because you exist. You will enjoy mental well-being if you adopt this attitude, and this can endure in the hereafter if this is your belief! Alternatively, you may deem yourself valuable since you are a human being, which will also be effective, assuming you do not become non-human or an android! However, there can be difficulties with these standpoints since someone could state that they regard you as worthless because you exist or are a human being. Your resolve to deem yourself valuable as a consequence of your existence or that you are a human being is, accordingly, grounded in your conviction. If you are capable of upholding your conviction, you will enjoy mental well-being.

Desisting from assigning your 'self' a universal grading is, in my opinion, a more practical and beneficial stance—but it is also more taxing. Here, you acknowledge that human beings' intricacy and complexity prohibit assigning a universal grading and that it would be an unmitigated oversimplification if you gave such a rating to yourself and you would unjustly typify yourself in doing so. Alternatively, you can unconditionally accept yourself as an intricate and imperfect individual with positive, negative and neutral characteristics. In this way, you can endeavour to strengthen your positive attributes and curtail your negative attributes, although these will never be eliminated. However, it is important to note that it is impossible to become an expert in this unconditional self-acceptance attitude since we have an inherent tendency to make unjustified over-simplifications and, in particular circumstances, to transmute a grading of one of our attributes into a grading of our entire selves. We can more reasonably seek to curtail (instead of eradicate) our proclivity to self-rate and to strengthen (instead of perfect) our tendency to accept ourselves unconditionally.

I want to re-emphasise my point from Principle 1 that acceptance is not the equivalent of submission or resignation. By urging you to accept yourself unconditionally as an imperfect individual, I am not suggesting you resign yourself to who you are in respect of not endeavouring to modify your counter-productive attributes and strengthen those qualities that enrich your life. Assuming an unconditional self-acceptance attitude enables you to attempt to reshape yourself rather than adopt a submissive or a despondent position.

Appreciate Your Uniqueness

Integral to being human is the fact that you are a *unique* and *distinctive* person. There will never again exist an individual with the array of attributes, capabilities, aptitudes and limitations that you possess. When I present to an audience on develop-ing a healthy attitude to yourself, I suggest that there will doubtless never be another person with the same combination of interests as me. For instance, I enjoy listening to soul music, especially Junior Walker and The All Stars; I love the music and performances of Al Jolson; I am a fan of the Marx Brothers; I enjoy watching professional boxing broadcasts; I support Arsenal Football Club; I am fond of reading Billy Bunter novels; and I am dedicated to writing about psychotherapy and emotional self-help. I think it is improbable that you will encounter another person with that same mix of interests. Therefore, I can either appreciate my uniqueness or regard myself as bizarre or an oddball. I choose to appreciate my uniqueness since it is more sensible, true to life and healthier. Accordingly, I suggest you contemplate your innumerable individual qualities and appreciate your uniqueness.

At one time, I was under the impression that there were particular pastimes or hobbies that I absolutely should or shouldn't have. Therefore, I thought that I *absolutely should* enjoy attending the opera and art galleries and *absolutely shouldn't* enjoy professional boxing or game shows on the television. Accordingly, I felt guilty about enjoying particular pastimes and I rejected my uniqueness. This is no longer the case since I am now firmly convinced that a person should ideally pursue any interest enthusiastically—assuming it has no negative impact on others or nature—regardless of whether others dismiss or ridicule it. Therefore, if you enjoy playing marbles or adding to your coin collection, go ahead and partake in these activities and seek to share them with others of the same mind. It is important not to succumb to the notion that you *absolutely shouldn't* enjoy particular pastimes, since that would be destructive to the self, nonsensical and unrealistic. Permit and empower yourself to participate wholeheartedly in your genuine interests and hobbies.

Also, appreciate your unique array of attributes. Be aware of your character traits and locate situations in which you can demonstrate these and, assuming it is not to your detriment to do so, steer clear of conditions which restrict the demonstration of your character traits. This is of particular signif-icance when deciding on your profession, employ-ment or calling. For instance, if you are extroverted, it would be undesirable for you to pursue an occupation that may prevent you from demonst-rating that characteristic, such as a researcher, software engineer or a landscaper. Further, if you are an introvert, it may be undesirable for you to seek a role that requires a great deal of socialising or exuberance, such as in politics, event planning or sales. Therefore, it is valuable to be aware of your character traits to enable you to form a considered judgment regarding which situations would best allow you to demonstrate them—although there are always exceptions. You may wish to consider seek-ing guidance on this from a reputable careers consultant, who will help you determine professions that will enable you to demonstrate your distinctive array of attributes (and interests).

Develop the Principle of Self-Care

It is crucial, and an indicator of mental well-being, to position your interests above those of others. You may be able to find someone who will place your interests above their own, but this is problematic since they will hold a very dim view of themselves, be dependent on you and be very eager to please. Essentially, you will become aware that the relationship is very limited and confined.

I am certainly not encouraging you to become self-centred, which would mean you lack consideration for other people and presume they will conform to your self-centred habits and are concerned chiefly with your benefit. In terms of the principle of 'self-care', I am suggesting you consider your interests whilst also being mindful of the interests of those with whom you are in relationships and ensuring you respect your commitments to them. I am not even suggesting that the interests of others will always be subordinate to your own; in fact, you may sometimes position the needs of others above your own, especially those of your children. It has recently been suggested that children may thrive when they discern their parents healthily considering their interests, rather than making them inferior to their children's interests. Therefore, the crux of self-care is adaptability. Fundamentally, you are considering your interests in a manner that is adaptable and reasonable to the circumstances' requirements, but which is not self-centred and does not disregard others' interests.

Establishing and preserving healthy boundaries is crucial to self-care. Every individual should preferably take care of themself physically (this will be examined below) and emotionally and allocate time for healthy private contemplation. It is important to bear this in mind, in light of the many connections you have with important people in your life. Additionally, you are likely to be accountable and answerable for various responsibilities in your work. Furthermore, you may participate in various leisure activities or pastimes. Therefore, it is crucial to establish healthy boundaries and restrictions; otherwise, you may become overloaded and neglect your physical and emotional health and your desire for private contemplation.

To achieve mental well-being, my recommendation is to review all your tasks and interests and formulate a means to undertake each one. This will require some prioritisation to apportion adequate time to these tasks and interests. It will also require you to manage your time productively, which is another indicator of emotional well-being.

As a case in point, one of my clients, Jacob, asserted that his wife and children were of the most significant importance in his life. However, when we examined the amount of time he devoted to them compared to his career, friends, and pastimes, he was astonished that his family occupied only a small proportion of his time. As is typical, his perception was that since he loves his family, it was unnecessary to devote much time to them. I assisted Jacob in rescheduling his life to dedicate more time to those things of most significance. He needed to restrict his interactions with some others and sacrifice some enjoyable interests; however, by apportioning his time in line with his preferences and establishing healthy boundaries, he became healthier and more content while actualising his values.

It is a cliché to state that we only live once; however, it is common for people to behave as if life goes on forever. If you behave this way, you may say, 'I will do that another time.' However, you may have to face the disparity between those things you consider to be of utmost importance and your lifestyle at times when you are reminded of your mortality, such as sustaining a life-threatening injury or illness. We frequently read accounts of people who have entirely re-evaluated and reframed their lives following a severe injury or illness. However, it is possible to re-evaluate your life without experiencing a life-threatening event! You can examine what you regard to be of utmost importance, establish healthy boundaries around your tasks and interests and opt for a life that is consistent with your values and priorities. It is certainly worth consideration.

Respect Your Commitments to Yourself

Many of us are vulnerable to positioning others and tasks ahead of ourselves. We may have ambitions to live abroad or start a business, for instance. We may dedicate ourselves to these ambitions; however, we frequently fail to respect our commitments to ourselves and fail to take steps to achieve them. We have all heard people declare, 'If I could live my life over again, I would do so many things differently.' Bleak as it may seem, it may be worthwhile to visualise yourself at the end of your life and consider what 'if onlys' you may be thinking. Write these down and aspire to respect your commitments to yourself from now on. You will probably be unable to achieve all that you wish to; it will be necessary to accept this fact—avoid the 'if only' trap—and prioritise goals and tasks. You may have to concede that you may not achieve some of your less important goals. Nevertheless, determine to dedicate yourself to the goals you consider most important and worthwhile and respect these commitments.

Establish a Healthy Attitude to Your Physical Well-Being

It is often suggested that you cannot achieve mental well-being without physical well-being. However, this is not entirely accurate. I am aware of several people who have been afflicted with debilitating diseases, but then appear to be motivated by this to attain great strength of will and determination and, ultimately, achieve mental well-being—more so than if they had not suffered from the illness. However, if you lack physical fitness, your energy and drive may diminish, and the resulting apathy makes it is more arduous to strive progressively for better emotional health.

It is important to appreciate the need to be attentive to your body and physical health. I would like to reassure you that I do not intend to counsel you about the detrimental effects of various vices, such as smoking and drinking. I do not wish to deter you from reading on! I also do not intend to counsel you on the value of signing up for gym membership or taking part in regular physical activity. I do not want to do this, first, because I am not qualified to do so and, second, since I do not wish to lecture you.

Nevertheless, I would like to emphasise that it is vital for you to have *some* regard for your physical health; otherwise, you will probably subsequently be more at risk of physical decline, which may precipitate deterioration in your mental health.

As in other areas, it is important to adopt a flexible approach to physical activity—it being neither excessive nor non-existent—and I would recommend seeking guidance from your general practitioner and possibly a nutritionist in developing a balanced diet and exercise regime to promote sound long-term physical health.

Further, I would recommend you become knowledgeable regarding any potential fragilities in your health and initiate any practical or protective action advised by specialists. We commonly live in a manner that suggests we are not susceptible to stroke, cancer or other serious diseases. We only make adaptations to our way of life after being ill. Therefore, consider what balanced action you can take—without becoming obsessive or adopting an untested and dubious new craze—to protect yourself from illness. It is impossible to preclude every disease, but some minor protective action now may well be far less unfavourable than enduring medical procedures in the future.

Understand How to Nurture Yourself

Nurturing yourself indicates that you should behave towards yourself as you would towards a loved one. Remarkably, we are often educated about and presented with frameworks that illustrate how individuals nurture others. However, this seldom extends to being educated about or presented with frameworks that demonstrate how individuals nurture themselves. To illustrate, I will outline an example of how I nurture myself. I find it very relaxing to watch model railway videos on YouTube, and I devote a short amount of time everyday to watching these. You may not be of the same mind, and I would not suggest this would be a nurturing experience for everyone! I recommend that you contemplate which pastimes or ventures are soothing for you and in which you can frequently engage. As already mentioned in this book, individuals enjoy a diversity of activities and what we consider as nurturing will differ. Therefore, it is essential to determine what you can do with other people, alone or what others can do for you that you consider nurturing and participate in these frequently; whether this is meditating or taking a long walk, for example. The effect on your emotional health will astonish you.

Endeavour to Achieve Your Standards, Values and Morals

Do not be alarmed; I do not intend to lecture you! However, I do wish to suggest that you contemplate your standards, values, and morals and endeavour to achieve them. As human beings, we are all prone to failing to do this occasionally. In these circumstances, I urge you to have faith in yourself and learn from 'failure'.

Nevertheless, in my opinion, the most contented individuals live in harmony with their standards, values and morals, since they have a perception that they are assisting in shaping a world in which they desire to exist. Also, they appear to be more at ease with themselves than those who habitually contradict that which they hold in high regard in respect of values and morals. Should you struggle to discern your values, you may like to refer to Simon, Howe and Kirschenbaum's book, *Values Clarification* (Warner Books, 1995).

Endeavour to Be Genuine

In this complicated, modern, day-to-day world, it is tough to be authentic. Sociologists argue that we are continually pressurised to play a part, hide behind a mask or veil or conceal our real feelings to attain greater productivity. I cannot deny that these infl-uences exist. Nevertheless, I consider it possible to be reasonably genuine despite encountering these pressures.

I will examine two types of genuineness. First, I will discuss being genuine with yourself. Here, you are truthful with yourself and do not attempt to conceal your real feelings in pointlessly striving to achieve an unrealistic utopian vision of a human— the most expeditious course to becoming alienated from your genuine feelings. It will be considerably simpler to be truthful with yourself if you have made strides in developing the unconditional self-accept-ance attitude that I discussed earlier in this principle. Therefore, it may be beneficial to reconsider this before reading on. Presuming you possess a reasonable degree of unconditional self-acceptance, it is necessary to heed your feelings and genuine values, thoughts, beliefs and attitudes. Undertake not to persuade yourself that you are anybody different from who you are. Those who have achieved harmony with themselves concede their short-comings and may take purposeful, but untroubled steps to tackle them. Yet those who are in conflict with themselves refute their shortcomings, attribute them to other people or frantically attempt to modify them.

It is also important to be genuine with other people. Truthfully divulging those things that you favour and those you do not, especially at the start of a relationship, can avert much anguish and wasted effort. Can you recall instances when you have put on a front because you assume people would reject you if you were truthful with them? A Jesuit priest named John Joseph Powell wrote an excellent book in 1972 entitled *Why Am I Afraid to Tell You Who I Am?* In the book, he discusses that—peculiar as it sounds—a deficiency of unconditional self-acceptance of our faults is at the core of our dread of being genuine with other people. It is more probable that you will be real with other people if you accept yourself unconditionally. If someone does not accept you, it would be disappointing. Still, it would be less upsetting at the start of a relationship than if you concealed your genuine feelings and suffered rejection much later upon disclosing them.

I am not proposing that you be heartless, insensitive and discourteous to other people. It is possible to reveal and sensitively convey decidedly negative feelings. I do not recommend taking an immature all-holds-barred shouting and shrieking approach to being genuine, since this would be unhealthy for all parties concerned. It is important that you convey your feelings genuinely, but with respect and sensitivity. As in other matters, it is necessary to be flexible in demonstrating your genuineness!

*

When you face life's adversities and adopt one or more of the four attitudes that I discussed in the previous four principles, then, you will experience what I call 'healthy negative emotions'. This may sound strange, but, as I will argue in the following principle, feeling bad, but not disturbed about one of life's adversities is a hallmark of good mental health.

PRINCIPLE 6

Feel Bad, But Not Disturbed

Since this book seeks to help you develop good mental health, it may seem peculiar to have a section concerning experiencing negative emotions. Nevertheless, it is important that you dispel any assumptions you have that mentally healthy individuals only experience positive feelings and are composed and poised in the face of negative experiences. This is an overly idealistic notion of mental well-being. If anyone were to experience purely positive emotions, they would either never have been confronted with misfortune or their positive responses would be incongruous with the misfortune they experience. Since your feelings stem from your attitudes, individuals who feel positive regarding a negative experience do so due to an unrealistic, positive attitude towards the experience.

For instance, imagine you are a participant in a photography competition and have been selected as a finalist. You are very keen to win since the competition is of great consequence to you and you are very excited. However, the competition organisers send you a letter informing you that you did not win. Wouldn't it be unrealistic for you to possess the attitude, 'I'm happy that I didn't win the competition'? You would need to possess this attitude to have positive feelings regarding the event. It is perfectly acceptable to possess both positive and negative feelings towards the event; for instance, 'I am unhappy that I didn't win the competition, although I am glad that I was a finalist.' Your attitude, 'I am unhappy that I didn't win the competition', would engender displeasure, but this is a healthy negative emotion. It is undoubtedly disagreeable to feel this negative emotion, although it is beneficial since it empowers you to adapt to the negative experience, process it and move forward.

Now imagine that you feel unconcerned or nonchalant that you have not won the competition. This would also not demonstrate mental well-being, since each individual holds an intricate array of preferences, as examined in Principle 2. Therefore, there are certain things that you want to happen and others you would prefer not to occur. When a disagreeable event occurs, such as discovering that you have not won the photography competition, this represents a thwarting of your aspirations. It is, therefore, healthy to experience negative feelings such as displeasure.

To experience no feelings (for example, feeling unconcerned and nonchalant) regarding the competition loss, you would need to hold an attitude that supports this feeling—or absence of feeling. Your underlying attitude would have to be that winning or losing the competition was unimportant to you. Here, you would be deluding yourself, or this would be what psychologists would term a case of the mechanism of denial. When you hold an attitude of indifference, you are acting like the fox in the story of the fox and the grapes. If you recall, the fox really wanted the grapes, but could not reach them. Rather than healthily concluding that this was a disappointing experience and that maybe he needed to give some more thought to solving the problem of reaching the grapes, the fox decided that he didn't want the grapes anyway since they were very likely to be sour.

I expect it will be apparent to you why healthy negative emotions are an indicator of mental well-being. Experiencing purely positive emotions would signify that you feel positively regarding negative experiences, which is an unrealistic stance. Feeling nonchalant regarding your aspirations suggests you are deluding yourself and refuting those things of most significance to you.

The remainder of this principle will examine healthy negative emotions and demonstrate how these are underpinned by the healthy attitudes explored in Principles 2 to 5. These will be contrasted with unhealthy negative emotions underpinned by unhealthy attitudes, which were also examined in the earlier principles. I will summarise these sections here, although if you require more comprehensive information regarding healthy and unhealthy attitudes, you may wish to review the above-mentioned principles before proceeding.

In my opinion, the healthy negative emotions that will be examined in a moment originate from one or more of the attitudes below:

- Flexibility;
- A non-awfulising attitude coupled with an acceptance of reality;
- An attitude of discomfort tolerance; and
- An unconditional acceptance towards oneself, others and life conditions.

Unhealthy negative emotions, on the other hand, originate from one or more of the attitudes below:

- Rigid demands;
- An awfulising attitude that leads you to blow things out of proportion;
- An attitude of discomfort intolerance which leads to you pursuing short-term pleasure at the expense of your long-term healthy goals; and
- An attitude of devaluation towards oneself, others and life conditions.

In this principle, I will illustrate my point by discussing five healthy negative emotions:

1. Concern as opposed to anxiety
2. Sadness as opposed to depression
3. Healthy anger as opposed to unhealthy anger
4. Remorse as opposed to guilt and
5. Sorrow as opposed to hurt and self-pity

Concern (as Opposed to Anxiety)

If there is a threat to your welfare, health, comfort or perception of yourself, it is healthy to be concerned about this threat. Trying to ignore the threat risk or pretending it is not real will not help challenge and manage it; neither will falling to pieces and becoming overwhelmingly anxious. Concern is rooted in the ideology that if a threat is present, all the conditions, regrettably, exist for it to be so. It would be more agreeable if it were not present; however, there is no law of the universe which states that it must not exist. Besides, the existence of the threat may be unpleasant, although not terrible. Someone with good mental well-being may think, 'I can tolerate this experience and manage the threat risk if and when it transpires, and if it does, I can accept myself unconditionally in such conditions.'

The harmful equivalent to concern in confronting a threat is anxiety. If you feel anxious about a threat, you demand that it must not transpire; if it did, you think it would be terrible and that you would be unable to tolerate it, and if the threat was to your perception of yourself and it happened, it would demonstrate that you had no value.

It is healthy to feel concerned regarding a threat since:

- It assists in recognising the reality of a threat; and

- It facilitates logical and coherent thinking and encourages you to manage the threat practically should it transpire or, if the threat cannot be abolished, to develop other ideas that enrich or improve your life.

Furthermore, feeling concerned instead of anxious deems it less probable that you will exaggerate the level of threat; in fact, I have undertaken research that demonstrates the veracity of this.

During one investigation, I requested that a group of research subjects hold a set of flexible and non-extreme attitudes towards spiders. These subjects were asked to possess the attitude: 'I would prefer not to see a spider, but that does not mean that I must not do so. If I do, it would be unfortunate but not terrible. It is uncomfortable seeing a spider but not unbearable.' Another group of research subjects was asked to possess a set of rigid and extreme attitudes towards spiders. They were asked to believe the following: 'I must not see a spider. If I were to see one, it would be horrible and unbearable.' Each group of subjects was requested to imagine that they would be entering a room where there would be at least one spider, and they were asked several questions regarding how many spiders may be in the room, what size they may be and in which direction they may be moving.

You may have predicted that the group with rigid and extreme attitudes regarding spiders hypothesised that a more significant number of larger spiders would be moving in their direction than the group with flexible and non-extreme attitudes. This investigation demonstrates that possessing an unhealthy anxiety-associated attitude generates an exaggeration of the risk level in a situation. Also, there will be a propensity to under-estimate your capacity to manage the risk. Yet, if you feel unanxious concern, you neither exaggerate the threat nor underestimate your ability to manage it.

Sadness (as Opposed to Depression)

When you experience the loss of someone or something significant to you, such as someone you love, a pet or your job, it is healthy to experience sadness regarding the loss. Attempting to disregard the loss as if you are indifferent to it will not help you process the loss, pick yourself up, and move forward with your life. It is also unhealthy to experience depression in respect of the loss since this inhibits action and gives rise to you becoming emotionally stuck.

Sadness about a loss (or a failure) stems from the idea that it is undesirable for the loss to have occurred, but no law of the universe states that it absolutely shouldn't have happened. If it happened, it happened. It is bad that the loss occurred, but not terrible. It is bearable and does not reflect on your worth as a person.

However, if you are depressed about the loss (or failure), you likely hold that the loss absolutely should not have happened, that it is terrible and unbearable and proves something worthless about you.

If you experience sadness—but not depression—in respect of a loss (or failure), you do not experience hopelessness regarding the future, since you discern that loss is a component of the intricacy of life and that it is essential to amalgamate this into a broad perspective of the world. If you experience depression, you are inclined to feel hopeless regarding the future and in an extreme case to consider suicide. Since you do not acknowledge that such losses (and failures) should transpire, life loses all meaning.

Sadness helps you mourn and move forward and empowers you to take practical action; whereas depression has a propensity to hinder or prolong mourning. Furthermore, depression leads you to feel incapable of action, and any action you take will probably not be productive. Therefore, it is undoubtedly important to experience sadness in respect of losses and failures; however, attempt to curtail feelings of depression by recognising and examining the rigid and extreme attitudes underpinning this unhelpful negative emotion.

Healthy Anger (as Opposed to Unhealthy Anger)

If someone frustrates you, threatens your perception of yourself or contravenes one of your fundamental personal rules, it would be unhealthy to condone and absolve them of their actions, demonstrate goodwill or ignore their conduct. Instead, in my opinion, it is healthy to be healthily angry when such a disagreeable situation occurs. If a trusted friend breaks your confidence, would it be healthy to condone and ignore their behaviour? Certainly not. I consider it very healthy to experience anger towards your friend's actions and attempt to remedy the situation constructively.

If you experience healthy anger—a healthy negative emotion—it is underpinned by the attitudes below:

- 'It would be preferable for such frustrations, etc. not to occur, but that does not mean that they must not occur';
- 'It is quite unfortunate when they occur, but not terrible';
- 'It is a struggle to tolerate this situation, but I can tolerate it, and it is worth it to me to do so. I am willing to tolerate this, and I am going to do so'; and
- 'The other person who has frustrated me is a person who has acted in a bad manner but is not a bad person. They are fallible.'

In contrast, unhealthy anger—often at the core of relational discord and a destroyer rather than enhancer of relationships—derives from the rigid and extreme attitudes below:

- 'The other person absolutely must not break my rules or frustrate me';
- 'It is terrible that they did';
- 'The situation is unbearable'; and

- 'The other person is a bad person for acting in such a bad manner.'

Experiencing and exhibiting unhealthy anger will increase your blood pressure and generate further conflict with the individual in question. They will encounter you as criticising them instead of feeling distaste for their actions. Also, they will likely want vengeance, even if they feel overawed by you. However, should you not convey your unhealthy anger, you will also experience difficulties in the form of an array of psychosomatic symptoms. You may seek to retaliate in a passive-aggressive manner and experience an overall sense of disquiet and disturbance.

Yet, if you feel healthy anger, it is more probable that you will take practical measures to effect change by initiating a discussion with the individual. You truthfully elucidate your feelings regarding their actions, whilst being clear that you are not criticising them as a person. You hope to settle the matter and maintain your friendship or rapport and accept them as an imperfect human being.

Therefore, if someone frustrates you as you strive to achieve your aspirations, endangers your perception of yourself or contravenes one of your rules, do not ignore or condone their actions. Instead, feel healthy anger and attempt to take practical steps to rectify the situation.

Remorse (as Opposed to Guilt)

Can you recall a time when you have fallen short of a code of ethics or a moral value or behaved in a manner that is contradictory to your principles? The majority—or possibly all—of us have, and most people consider guilt a healthy response. By precisely interpreting guilt and differentiating it from its healthy and beneficial equivalent—remorse—it becomes evident that guilt is not a useful or healthy reaction to circumstances in which you lapse from your moral code. Guilt originates from the attitude that: 'I absolutely must not break my moral code, fail to live up to my moral values or hurt someone's feelings. If I do so, it is terrible, I cannot stand the situation and I am a bad, wicked sinner for so doing.' If you possess this attitude, it will inspire poor behaviour later on, since if it is accurate that you are a bad and wicked individual, how else would you behave other than badly and wickedly?

I would like to clarify that I certainly am not disregarding wrongdoing. If you contravene your code of ethics or moral values or cause suffering to another, it is healthy to experience remorse, and, should you do so, you will possess the attitudes that follow:

- 'I acted badly (by breaking my ethical code, failing to live up to my moral values or hurting someone's feelings) and I wish that I hadn't. However, there is no law in the universe which states that I must not act badly';
- 'This situation is bad and calls for me to reflect on what I've done. However, it is not terrible';
- 'It is uncomfortable to act badly, but it's not unbearable'; and
- 'I am a fallible human being who did the wrong thing, but I am not a bad person.'

In my opinion, possessing these attitudes, which are at the core of constructive remorse, will influence you to contemplate your actions and enhance the probability that you will learn from your errors. If you feel guilty—and therefore blame yourself—you will either refute any culpability for your actions, or your wrongdoing will completely absorb you and you will therefore be unable to learn from your mistakes.

Consequently, be aware that you will sometimes fall short of your moral principles and virtues since you are an imperfect individual. It is important to accept yourself unconditionally as a flawed individual, permit feelings of remorse, gain knowledge from your mistakes and make reparations for your actions. Refrain from reprehending yourself as an undeserving, immoral wrongdoer. This will serve only to inspire further poor behaviour, as you fulfil your 'wrongdoer' role or because you fail to learn from your errors due to your burden of guilt.

Sorrow (as Opposed to Hurt or Self-Pity)

As demonstrated in my book *The Incredible Sulk* (Sheldon Press, 1992), sulking predominantly comprises feeling hurt and self-pitying. If you are feeling hurt and self-pitying, you will be inclined to possess these attitudes in respect of the unjust or unwarranted conduct you have received:

- 'Because I don't deserve unfair treatment it absolutely must not happen'; and
- 'Because I have been mistreated it is terrible, I can't bear it, and the world is a rotten place for allowing this to happen to such an undeserving creature like me.'

Do you consider that feeling hurt and self-pitying assists in practically managing injustice? In my experience, it is more probable that those who feel hurt and self-pitying disengage from beneficial or useful interactions instead of entering into them. They are inclined to sulk or to converse with other people in a pessimistic, judgmental style. Further, there may be attempts to evoke sympathy and pity from their loved ones, which, if achieved, will amplify their self-pitying attitude.

What is a more useful possibility than feeling hurt and self-pitying? The alternative is sorrow since it is healthy to experience sorrow if you have received unjust conduct, which you consider unwarranted. It is important to differentiate between sorrow on the one hand and hurt and self-pity on the other. If you feel hurt and self-pity, you consider yourself a poor soul for experiencing this conduct; however, if you feel sorrow, but not self-pity, you consider yourself to be in an unfortunate situation, but not that you should be pitied as a person. Moreover, if you experience sorrow, but not hurt and self-pity, it is probable that your attitude is as follows:

- 'While it is undesirable to be treated in an unfair, undeserving manner, there is no law

of the universe that says that fairness and
deservingness must exist';

- 'If the unfairness exists, then it is bad but not
  terrible';
- 'It is a situation that I can stand and therefore
  can try to correct'; and
- 'The world is hardly a rotten place but is a
  complex environment in which bad and good
  things happen; it is a place where, if I think
  about it, I experience certain unfairnesses
  which are in my favour.'

The final point is significant. The majority of
those who read this book probably enjoy good
health, are of sound mind and have all their limbs
intact. Would this not be unjust for those suffering
ill-health, who are not of sound mind or have lost
limbs? When we concentrate on injustices that are to
our advantage, it is doubtful that we will demand
that these should not exist! Therefore, in feeling hurt
and self-pity we unduly concentrate on injustices
against us and disregard or entirely spurning justices
that are to our advantage.

To conclude, I would like to re-emphasise that it
is unhealthy to put on a front and only acknowledge
positive aspects of the situation when you encounter

adverse circumstances. Also, it is unhealthy to affect an attitude of detachment and nonchalance. Instead, when you experience adverse circumstances, it is healthy to feel concerned, sad, healthy anger, remorse or sorrow; there is no need to attempt to modify these feelings. Suppose you permit yourself to experience these feelings. In that case, they will help you practically manage the circumstances and become healthily accustomed to them, if it is impossible to effect change. Nevertheless, should you feel anxious, depressed, unhealthy anger, guilt and hurt or self-pity, examine the rigid and extreme attitudes that form the basis of such feelings and modify them to strive to replace them with healthy negative emotions.

*

This book is partly about you understanding what to do to develop good mental health, particularly in the face of life's adversities. However, it is also about you applying this understanding. So, in the following and final principle, I will discuss what I call a realistic approach to personal change and outline the steps that you can take to develop good mental health.

PRINCIPLE 7

Be Realistic About Personal Change

An essential feature of establishing good mental well-being is adopting a realistic approach towards individual change and implementing it. This final principle will outline nine steps that it will be necessary to work through to initiate a feasible programme of personal change.

Step 1: Acknowledge that You Have a Problem and Accept Yourself Unconditionally for Having It

If you are unwilling to acknowledge that you have a problem, it will not be easy to effect change in respect of it. Shame can be an obstacle to acknowledging that you have a problem since your attitude is that, 'If I disclose this problem, it will demonstrate that I am valueless, inept, feeble and helpless.' If this is your attitude, then it is simpler to refute any difficulties and condemn others for you having them than to acknowledge that you have a

99

problem. Therefore, accepting yourself unconditionally for having a problem is critical in admitting that you have it. In Principle 5, I demonstrated that a crucial characteristic of mental well-being is establishing an attitude of unconditional self-acceptance. You do not consider that your worth as a person varies according to whether or not you have an emotional problem. If you acknowledge that you have a problem, doing so will facilitate you to take responsibility for it, which will empower you to transition to the next part of your change programme.

Step 2: Be Precise

It is not easy to surmount problems of indistinct character. Therefore, be abundantly precise in defining your problem and examining examples of it.

Step 3: Identify your Disturbed Emotion

The greater the precision in identifying your disturbed emotion, the more probable it is that you will understand that about which you are most disturbed. Attempt to steer clear of using vague phrases such as 'I feel agitated' or 'I feel upset'. It is also important to understand that some negative emotions are healthy; for instance, sadness as a reaction to loss, concern as a reaction to threat or healthy anger as a reaction to frustration (see Principle 6). Since these emotions are healthy, they are not problems. Nevertheless, if you consider them as such, you likely possess an attitude that you absolutely must not experience negative emotions in these situations. For instance, you may hold that you must be calm when facing a threat or that you should soldier on through a loss and turn a blind eye to an offence. Therefore, be sure to note down feelings such as anxiety, depression, hurt, guilt, unhealthy anger and self-pity, all of which are both negative and harmful.

Step 4: Identify the Feature of the Situation about Which You Are Most Disturbed

When you experience a negative, disturbed emotion (as noted above), it is vital to concentrate on what you are most disturbed about. In certain circumstances, there may be several features about which you are disturbed. Therefore, the greater the precision with which you determine the element about which you are, for instance, most anxious, the greater the degree to which you will be able to help yourself.

For example, let's assume that you feel anxious regarding public speaking—perhaps in case you freeze; possibly for fear of making a mistake; or perhaps in case the audience asks a question you cannot answer or openly criticises you. The greater your concentration on that about which you are most disturbed, the better. Therefore, consider the question, 'Which element of the situation am I most anxious about?' This will be the feature towards which it will be necessary to establish a new healthy attitude.

It will occasionally be apparent that the most troubling feature is distorted. For instance, you may determine that you fear that your audience will leave suddenly. Although this is highly improbable, it is critical, for now, to presume this will occur, since it is your fear. This will facilitate you to determine your unhelpful rigid and extreme attitudes which comprise Step 5.

Step 5: Determine your Rigid and Extreme Attitudes

There are four rigid and extreme attitudes which form the basis of a great deal of human emotional disturbance, as discussed in Principles 2 to 5:

- A rigid attitude—you maintain that you, others and the world must exist in a particular way;

- An awfulising attitude—you maintain that it would be awful, terrible dreadful and the end of the world if the circumstances that you contend must exist do not transpire;

- An attitude of discomfort intolerance—you maintain the attitude that you would be unable to tolerate the circumstances you contend must not transpire. You would either die instantly or nevermore feel contentment; and

- A devaluation attitude towards yourself, others and/or life conditions—you maintain, for instance, that you have less value in particular situations. If someone obstructs you, for example, they are despicable and reprehensible.

Seek the existence of one or more of these rigid/extreme attitudes and acknowledge that these attitudes are fundamentally responsible for your disturbed emotions.

Step 6: Examine Your Rigid and Extreme Attitudes

There are three key approaches to examining a rigid and extreme attitude. First, you can ask questions regarding how much the attitude complies with real life; for example, 'Is it a fact that I have to be successful?' and 'Is there a rule of the universe that deems it essential that I am successful?' There is only one right answer to these questions: 'No, there is no proof of either, since if there was, I would be compelled to succeed. I would be unable to violate such a law and, because none exist that determine that I must succeed, the only response to such questions is, "No, I do not have to be successful." Nevertheless, there is proof that I wish to succeed, although it's not essential—this is my flexible attitude. Therefore, I will cultivate my flexible attitude and detach from my rigid attitude.'

The second key approach to examining a rigid attitude is to ask questions regarding how logical the attitude is. For instance, you may possess the attitude, 'Since I wish for other people to take care of me, they absolutely must do so.' Does this verdict that they must do so logically derive from your wish for them to do so? Not at all. The following example that I mentioned in Principle 2 illustrates this. If I were to ask, 'Would you like to receive two thousand pounds instantly?' the majority of people would answer, 'Yes'. Then consider, 'So, since you wish to have this money, is it logical to conclude that you must receive it?' It is not, since what should occur does not logically derive from our wishes. This is acknowledged in your flexible attitude of 'I would like this to occur, but it is not essential that it does', which is logical, whereas the rigid attitude makes no logical sense. Therefore, once more, seek to cultivate your flexible attitude and detach from your rigid attitude.

The third key approach to examining rigid and extreme attitudes is possibly of greatest significance and concerns the repercussions of holding such an attitude. Therefore, it is important to consider: 'If I maintain the attitude that I must be certain regarding the results of my behaviour, what are the effects of possessing this attitude?' The effects are that you will experience anxiety and be hesitant and doubtful in making decisions. Nevertheless, if you maintain your flexible attitude that you wish to be certain regarding the outcome of your behaviour, but that this is not essential, this will empower you to feel healthy concern and to take practical measures to effect change.

To conclude, in the process of examining your flexible/non-extreme and rigid/extreme attitudes, consider the following three questions concerning each of your beliefs:

- Which attitude complies with reality, and which does not? Explain your selection.
- Which attitude is logical and which is not? Explain your selection.
- Which attitude generates the healthiest outcome? Explain your selection.

Further, you can consider which attitudes you would instil in your children and the reasons for that.

Step 7: Practice Will Strengthen Your Flexible/Non-Extreme Attitudes

To reiterate, the four principal flexible and non-extreme attitudes are:

- A flexible attitude;
- A non-awfulising attitude;
- An attitude of discomfort tolerance; and
- An attitude of unconditional acceptance in regards to the self, others and life conditions.

The fundamental element to acknowledge is that you will not begin to establish conviction in these new attitudes unless you frequently and enthusiastically behave in a manner compatible with these attitudes. If you only pursue your new flexible/non-extreme attitudes in a lukewarm, cursory fashion a couple of times a week, you will not establish conviction in them; yet, persistent, dedicated practice in behaving in accordance with them will. Therefore, dedicate yourself to such, whilst being vigilant of the five main traps that may prevent you from behaving in accordance with your new flexible/non-extreme attitudes in a dedicated and habitual way.

Trap 1: I am unable to take positive action until I feel comfortable

If you defer action until you feel comfortable, there will be a very long delay until positive action is taken. Therefore, behave in accordance with your new flexible and non-extreme attitudes despite feeling ill at ease in doing so. Feelings of comfort will develop later, following a great deal of practice.

Trap 2: I am unable to take positive action since I do not feel in control

Again, it is important to take action despite feeling a lack of control, since the intensity of your sense of control will increase in proportion with behaving in accordance with your new flexible and non-extreme attitudes.

Trap 3: I am unable to behave differently since I do not feel capable yet

Similarly, feelings of capability will develop from acting ineptly and gaining knowledge from your mistakes.

Trap 4: I am unable to act in new, unfamiliar ways, since I do not feel confident about doing so

Once more, the solution is taking action despite a lack of confidence.

Trap 5: I am unable to take constructive action, especially that which seems unsafe to me since I do not feel courageous enough to do so

Research on war heroes has demonstrated that fearlessness does not precede acts of courage. Anxiety is experienced by those who show courage and those who do not. The distinction is that those who are willing to behave bravely do not delay action until they feel courageous. Therefore, feel the fear and do it anyway.

Be aware that each of these traps starts with the letter 'c' — 'I will take action when I feel: comfortable, (in) control, capable, confident and courageous.' Alternatively, acknowledge that it would be pleasant if these five 'c's' were present, although none is essential and you can act in their absence.

Step 8: Generalise to Other Relevant Circumstances

When you have practised, for instance, dealing effectively with your need to be appreciated by yourwork colleagues, it is possible to generalise your new flexible/non-extreme attitudes—for example, 'I would like to be appreciated, but it's not essential' — to other circumstances where appreciation may cause problems for you, such as in your relationships with loved ones. These generalisations will not happen of their own accord—you will be required to incorporate them yourself.

Step 9: Preserve Your Gains

You may possess the mistaken notion that having undergone and been assisted by a self-improvement project, you have attained your objectives, and there is no need to make efforts to preserve your gains. Nevertheless, individuals tend to lapse and relapse unless they devote themselves to making continual efforts to protect such gains (which will be affirmed by anyone who has endeavoured to lose weight or stop smoking). Determining to practise strengthening your new flexible and non-extreme attitudes daily will generate gains later on.

To reduce the likelihood of lapses and relapses, it is necessary to prepare for them ahead of time. It is important to be especially aware of any personal vulnerabilities. For instance, you may be attempting to stop smoking, but have several friends who smoke. If you are susceptible to anxiety, your personal vulnerability may be crowded environments. The greater your ability to identify your personal vulnerabilities ahead of time and the greater your ability to discern, examine and modify the rigid/extreme attitudes that underpin these personal vulnerabilities, the greater your ability to reduce the likelihood of lapsing or relapsing.

It may be beneficial to steer clear of circumstances where you feel vulnerable at first until you have strengthened your flexible/non-extreme attitudes to a degree which enables you to tackle them success-fully. I would not wish you to feel overwhelmed, although it is important to become accustomed to healthily testing yourself. However, on account of being human, it is impossible to prevent lapses completely, although you will be much more likely to acquire knowledge from them if you can accept yourself unconditionally and dislike but not disturb yourself about lapses. If you are unduly disturbed regarding a setback or criticise yourself for one, you may eventually experience a relapse, and it will be necessary to start from scratch.

Conclusion

To conclude, it is important to acknowledge that preserving good mental well-being depends on dedicating yourself to making continual efforts to establish mental well-being and maintain it. Fort-unately, the more you do this, the easier it becomes. Besides, no one can ever achieve perfect mental well-being—not even me!

Good luck.

Index

113

Index

Lightning Source UK Ltd.
Milton Keynes UK
UKHW020632040221
378234UK00013B/1220